Introduction

In nearly six thousand pages of letters, reports, interviews, and memoirs, General George C. Marshall never makes a single mention of the military theorist Carl von Clausewitz.[1] This omission will not surprise Marshall scholars, as Marshall was not prone to either theorizing or waxing historic.[2] Nor will the omission surprise historians, as the dead Prussian was just one theorist among many who likely influenced Marshall.[3] Yet of twentieth century American generals, few understood Clausewitz's observation that "war is… a true political instrument" as well as George Marshall.[4] Avowedly and assiduously non-partisan, Marshall insisted on providing absolute candor to the commander in chief to enable his decision-making.[5] In appointing Marshall to shore up the American position in China, President Truman sought to leverage Marshall's understanding of the intersection of policy and war to both ensure Truman's

---

[1] George C. Marshall, *The Papers of George Catlett Marshall, Volumes I-VI*, eds. Larry I. Bland, Sharon Ritenour Stevens, Clarence E. Wunderlin, and Mark A. Stoler (Baltimore: The Johns Hopkins University Press, 1981-2013), hereafter cited as *PGCM vol. I-VI*; George C. Marshall, *Memoirs of My Services in the World War: 1917-1918* (Boston: Houghton Mifflin Company, 1976); George C. Marshall, *George C. Marshall: Interviews and Reminiscences for Forrest C. Pogue*, eds. Larry I. Bland and Joellen K. Bland (Lexington, VA: George C. Marshall Research Foundation, 1991), hereafter cited as *Marshall Interviews*.

[2] Marshall, *Marshall Interviews*, 161. One does not find much in the way of theory in the citations listed above, but in this interview Marshall speaks of his fear that at the outset of World War II "our officers were too theoretical." By this he meant that the officers did not have concrete experience, not that a theoretical education was detrimental.

[3] Thomas Bruscino, "Naturally Clausewitzian: U.S. Army Theory and Education from Reconstruction to the Interwar Years," *The Journal of Military History* 77 (October 2013): 1252. Others argue that the vernacular use of Clausewitz did not enter the US Army until three decades after Marshall left the service. See William J. Gregor, "Military Planning Systems and Stability Operations," *Prism* 1, no. 3 (June, 2010): 103.

[4] Carl von Clausewitz, *On War* (Princeton, NJ: Princeton University Press, 1976), 87.

[5] Mark A. Stoler, "The Marshall Legacy," in *George C. Marshall: Servant of the American Nation*, ed. Charles F. Browler (New York: Palgrave Macmillan, 2011): 178; David McCullough, *Truman* (New York, Simon & Schuster, 1992), 534.

1

intent would frame Marshall's actions and because Truman knew Marshall could accurately assess the warring parties in China.[6] Truman chose wisely.

After receiving the directive from President Truman to mediate a truce between the Communists and Nationalists in China in 1945, General George C. Marshall spent thirteen months attempting to implement a cease fire, a mechanism to monitor that cease fire, and a unified government and military.[7] But after an intense year where he and his small staff worked "10-14 hour war day[s]" trying every feasible means to bring the Nationalists and the Communists to an accord, Marshall assessed that the United States could not broker a peace and he ended the mission and withdrew the American contingent.[8] Then, ten months later as Secretary of State, George Marshall almost unilaterally blocked US military involvement in the Chinese civil war. When called to testify before the Senate and House in November of 1947, Marshall judged "that the Nationalists might lose the civil war" and US military involvement could become intractable.[9] In a frequently quoted passage at these same hearings, he stated that provision of effective support to Chiang Kai-shek and the Guomindang (GMD) would require "obligations and responsibilities… which I am convinced the American people would never knowingly accept."[10] When Marshall ceased mediation in January 1947 and prevented American entry into

---

[6] McCullough, *Truman*, 475.

[7] Katherine K. Reist, Review of *The Marshall Mission To China, 1945-1947: The Letters and Diary of Colonel John Hart Caughey*, ed. Roger Jeans, Journal of Military History 76, iss. 3 (July 2012): 921.

[8] John F. Melby, "The Marshall Mission in Retrospect," *Pacific Affairs* 50, no. 2 (Summer, 1977): 272. "War days" from John Hart Caughey, *The Marshall Mission to China, 1945-1947: The Letters and Diary of Colonel John Hart Caughey,* ed. Roger B. Jeans (Lanham, MD: Rowman & Littlefield Publishers, Inc., 2011), 21.

[9] Ernest R. May, "1947-48: When Marshall Kept the U.S. Out of War in China," *Journal of Military History* 66, iss. 4 (October, 2002): 1008-1009.

[10] Ibid., May cites from *Executive Sessions of the Committee on Foreign Relations, Historical Series,* 80th Cong., 2d sess., Session for 4 November 1947, 517-18. Though most of the primary source material employs the Wade-Giles system of transliteration from Chinese to

China's civil war ten months later, he did so in the face of enormous domestic pressure. The clamor for intervention came from the political right and left, from the military, and even from the ambassador to China that Marshall had helped to appoint. Furthermore, he knew that as an incipient Cold War dawned, many would judge his actions through the prism of communism's spread.[11] And yet Marshall remained undeterred and the United States never became involved in China's civil war.

As a result of his intransigence, some vilified Marshall as the man who lost China to the communists while others glorified Marshall as the man who saved the United States from an intractable quagmire.[12] The first narrative tells of a Marshall who did not do enough to empower the Nationalists and as a result lost China to the Communists. The second narrative focuses on his herculean efforts to bring peace and the difficult decision to forego further American involvement. Both narratives, though, focus on the actions he took to bring the warring parties to the negotiating table and the effects of withdrawing US support from Chiang Kai-shek and the GMD. Though the judgment of the effects differs in these narratives, the explanations in both narratives for why Marshall decided to withdraw from negotiations and proscribe military support to the Nationalists follow a similar pattern: Marshall made initial headway with the combatants, grew increasingly vexed with both the Chinese Communist Party (CCP) and the GMD, and, after determining that neither side truly wanted peace, made the decisions that either lost China to

---

English, I have employed *pinyin* as this is the more common transliteration system in use today. Where certain Wade-Giles transliterations are more familiar (Chiang Kai-shek rather than Jiang Jieshi for example), I have elected to employ Wade-Giles. I have given the Wade-Giles transliteration in parenthesis following the first use of the word or name.

[11] Ibid., 1007-1008.

[12] John Robinson Beal, *Marshall In China* (Garden City, NY: Doubleday, 1970), 365-367; Barry F. Machado, "Undervalued Legacy: Marshall's Mission to China," in *George C. Marshall: Servant of the American Nation,* ed. Charles F. Browler (New York: Palgrave Macmillan, 2011): 118.

3

communism or saved the United States and, in at least one account, Europe.[13] This monograph will not seek to debunk this explanation. In fact, primary documents support the narrative of Marshall's mounting frustration.[14] But if he knew how to do anything, George C. Marshall knew how to work through frustration.[15] He also knew, perhaps as well as anyone in the United States, the limits of military power writ large and, especially, the limits of American military power in China. This monograph will seek an explanation for why Marshall assessed that US military assistance to Chiang Kai-shek would not achieve US strategic objectives. Specifically, this monograph will seek to examine how operational considerations affected George Marshall's views on China after World War II.

The literature surrounding the Marshall Mission does not attempt to evaluate his decision either through the lens of an operational artist or through mission variables per se. Since the United States did not participate in a campaign in China after 1945, one should not expect to find discussions of lines of operation, basing, or other elements of operational art in the context of US military involvement in China. Moreover, almost immediately following the failure of Marshall's mission in China, President Truman appointed Marshall to Secretary of State.[16] Much of the literature thus focuses more on Marshall's vision in determining political objectives rather than how he evaluated and employed military force to pursue strategic objectives. Ernest R. May's superb essay titled "1947-1948: When Marshall Kept the U.S. Out of War in China" in the *Journal of Military History* falls into this category, as does Barry Machado's chapter in *George C.*

---

[13] Machado, "Undervalued Legacy," 123.

[14] John Hart Caughey, *The Marshall Mission to China, 1945-1947: The Letters and Diary of Colonel John Hart Caughey,* ed. Roger B. Jeans (Lanham, MD: Rowman & Littlefield Publishers, Inc., 2011), 21.

[15] Forrest C. Pogue, *George C. Marshall: Statesman* (New York: Viking Penguin, 1987), 225.

[16] Andrew Birtle, "The Marshall Mision: A Peacekeeping Mission that Failed," *Military Review* 80, iss. 2 (March/April 2000): 102.

Marshall: Servant to the American Nation.[17] Similarly, Mark Stoler's *George C. Marshall: Soldier-Statesman of the American Century* looks to the impact of the negotiations on Marshall's subsequent dealings with the Senate regarding China.[18] Forrest C. Pogue's account of Marshall in *George C. Marshall: Statesman* and Larry Bland's *George C. Marshall's Mediation Mission to China*, a compilation of twenty-four essays, offer critical context through which to view Marshall's papers from the period.[19] Colonel John Caughey's recently published papers (*The Marshall Mission to China, 1945-1947: The Letters and Diary of Colonel John Hart Caughey*) provide insight into the internal discussions and movements within the Marshall Mission. John Caughey served as an aide for Marshall throughout the negotiation mission and describes both the intensity of the effort and the frustration of dealing with obstinacy in the CCP and GMD. The most valuable inference from Caughey's letters comes in the impression that Marshall truly believed that his mission could succeed and that the US strategic end state of a strong, inclusive, and democratic China with Chiang Kai-shek at its helm was possible. This source aided in building an accurate time-line for Marshall's change in opinion that influenced his final assessment.

Marshall's service in China was not limited to the mission in 1946; in fact, Marshall served in China and wrote of his views during a tour in the 1920s. Indeed, George Marshall's experiences in China as an officer in the 1920s shaped his decisions in the 1940s. Marshall served as the executive officer and twice, temporarily, as commander of the 15th Tianjin (Tientsin)

---

[17] May, a professor of history at Harvard for fifty-five years, published fourteen books focused mainly on the United States from World War I on. Machado, a professor at Washington and Lee University, published two books, one focused on the Marshall Plan.

[18] Stoler, a professor of history at the University of Vermont, has written six books focused on US diplomatic and military history during World War II.

[19] During World War II, Forrest Pogue acted as an official US Army historian. He also directed the George Marshall Foundation. He and Larry Bland, the editor of the bulk of George Marshall's papers, comprise the foremost authorities on George Marshall.

Regiment from 1924 to 1927.[20] Primary source material from this period is not nearly as robust as during the later Marshall Mission, but Alfred Emile Cornebise's *The United States 15th Infantry Regiment in China, 1912-1938* provides excellent understanding into the routines, training events, and, most importantly, the uncertain operational environment in which Lieutenant Colonel Marshall operated at the 15th Infantry Regiment. Cornebise, a noted military historian, bases a great deal of his book on material drawn from *The Sentinel*, the weekly magazine produced by the 15th Infantry Regiment. Its poetry, stories, and non-fiction accounts provide color to the regiment's involvement in the events of the day and depict an interesting setting. Military historian Dennis Noble's treatment of many of the same sources in his book *The Eagle and the Dragon: The United States Military in China, 1901-1937* provide more detail for the context. Primary source material comes mainly from George Marshall's letters from his time in Tianjin. These not only act as a first-hand account, but since the focus of the monograph concerns Marshall's views, these letters describe the lessons that Marshall learned during his time in Tianjin. During Marshall's tenure at the 15th, he was faced with problems that required a thorough understanding of the operational environment. Given that he solved these problems, research into this period allows insight into how Marshall viewed the various conflagrations unfolding in China in the mid-1920s and, more importantly, the operational considerations for the 15th Infantry Regiment in Tianjin.

The final area of research concerns how Marshall viewed warfare in China and the mission variables attendant to that warfare. A combination of Marshall's correspondence, 15th Infantry Regiment intelligence estimates from his tour in the mid-twenties, and the correspondence from those individuals with whom Marshall had routine contact in China during his tours round out the assessment. Though he may not have referenced mission variables per se,

---

[20] Alfred Emile Cornebise, *The United State 15th Infantry Regiment in China, 1912-1938* (Jefferson, NC: McFarland & Company, Inc., Publishers), 36.

these sources indicate the considerations he deemed critical. The preeminent Marshall historian

Forrest C. Pogue's account of Marshall at the time offers one such consideration. Marshall

identified a "turning point" in negotiations when the Nationalists pushed the Communists out of

Siping (Szepingkai) because "it convinced the Nationalist generals that they could settle the

Manchurian problem by force."[21] Siping sits less than 200 kilometers North of Shenyang

(Mukden), the terminus of the Beijing (Peking) – Shenyang railway: the same railway that the

15th Infantry Regiment was charged with protecting during Marshall's tenure as executive

officer.[22] Marshall knew the importance of more than just terrain. Explication of these

considerations provides a lens through which to view his actions and statements regarding the

GMD in China. This monograph, then, fills a gap in the literature by looking George Marshall's

decisions in 1946 and 1947 through the operational lens gained in military service in China rather

than through a strategic lens of the early Cold War.

George C. Marshall spent thirteen months working with the Nationalists, Communists,

and other political stakeholders to bring about a negotiated settlement to the re-awakened Chinese

Civil War. Implicit in Marshall's attempt to convince Chiang Kai-shek and the GMD to

accommodate the Communists was a keen operational understanding of the GMD's ability to win

military victory over the Communists. Simply, Marshall knew, by virtue of the *coup d'oeil* gained

through decades of military experience, that the GMD could not defeat the Communists

militarily; it was this operational assessment that informed his decision to both end negotiations

and block a US military troop commitment to the Nationalists.[23] Support of this thesis requires a

---

[21] Pogue, *Marshall: Statesman*, 113.

[22] Cornebise, *15th Infantry Regiment*, 1.

[23] From the French "stroke of the eye," Carl von Clausewitz describes *coup d'oeil* "stripped of metaphor" as "the quick recognition of truth that the mind would ordinarily miss or would perceive only after long study and reflection." Carl von Clausewitz, *On War* (Princeton, NJ: Princeton University Press, 1976), 102.

methodology that will parse Marshall's *coup d'oeil* into the mission variables that would have informed his assessment.

This monograph will employ the framework of mission variables to examine why Marshall concluded that American operations in China would not support Truman's strategic intent of a negotiated peace.[24] Mission variables provide a filter to categorize relevant information in terms of mission, enemy, terrain, troops, time, and civil considerations to refine understanding of a situation.[25] The first section examines Marshall's first tour in China in depth. The section provides the context for the lessons Marshall learned and evaluates these lessons in detail. The second section evaluates Marshall's actions informed by the lessons he learned in his first tour. Evidence to inform these sections rests in the primary accounts written by members of the American and Chinese delegations taking part in the process during the period of negotiations. Primary sources from the period immediately following the Marshall Mission and in memoirs written after the fact aid in capturing Marshall's reasoning. Marshall did not make decisions in either a temporal or spatial vacuum: secondary sources aid in understanding the historical and geographic context for his decisions and discuss his time with the 15th Regiment in Tianjin (1924-1927). The criteria for evaluating possible answers to the question of Marshall's operational considerations include supportability from primary sources and the ability to place his reasoning in the context of decisions he made before and after his decision to end negotiations and prevent American involvement.

---

[24] While the mnemonic device METT-TC is anachronistic, mission variables are not.

[25] Army Doctrine Reference Publication (ADRP) 3-0, *Unified Land Operations* (Washington, DC: Government Printing Office, May 2012), 1-2.

Section One: Tianjin and Lessons Learned, 1924-1927

By the time he sailed for China in August 1924, Lieutenant Colonel George C. Marshall had a wealth of experience to draw on as the executive officer and commander of the 15th Infantry Regiment. Since his commission in 1902 – twenty-two years prior – Marshall served twice in the Philippines, he attended and instructed at the Command and General Staff School at Ft. Leavenworth, and he served as aide-de camp to three generals including a five-year term as aide to General John J. Pershing.[26] He also had a reputation for a preternatural capacity for large-unit movement and maneuver, a reputation gained while acting as an operations officer for the First Army as a temporary full colonel during the St. Mihiel and Meuse-Argonne campaigns of World War I.[27] When he arrived in China in on September 7, 1924, the anniversary of the Boxer Protocols of 1901, Marshall knew how to evaluate forces operating in a complex environment; a skill that he would hone during his tenure in the regiment.[28] This section examines the lessons Marshall learned during his three-year tour with the 15th Infantry and categorizes these lessons in terms of mission variables. Though Marshall himself did not parse his observations in terms of mission, troops, terrain, time, enemy, and civilian considerations, these categories provide a comprehensive structure to distill and display Marshall's thinking in the 1920s.[29] A common thread that runs through Marshall's observations during his time in the regiment concerns the limits of foreign power in the Middle Kingdom. The strands of this thread begin with the ambiguous nature of America's presence in China in the 1920s.

---

[26] Marshall, *Marshall Interviews*, ix-x.

[27] Stoler, *Marshall: Soldier-Statesman*, 86; Richard W. Stewart, ed., *American Military History, vol. II* (Washington, DC: US Army Center of Military History, 2010), 44.

[28] Marshall, *PGCM vol. I*, 263.

[29] ADRP 3-0, 1-2.

Mission

The historian Edward Coffman points out that during the 15th Infantry Regiment's time in Tianjin "most Americans, then and later, probably shared… unawareness that there was an Army unit stationed in China."[30] If unaware of its presence, even fewer Americans could have identified the unit's mission, not least because the regiment's higher headquarters – the United States Army Troops in China – never "succinctly prescribed in orders or clearly enunciated" a mission statement.[31] Part of the confusion stemmed from differences of opinion between the War Department and the Department of State, under whom the 15th Regiment fell after 1912, but the fundamental confusion came from the United States government's ambivalence towards the exercise of colonial power in China.[32] A brief review of the Boxer Rebellion and its aftermath illustrates this ambivalence.

In June 1900, the moribund Qing dynasty saw an opportunity to both harness domestic discontent and possibly expel encroaching Western powers by supporting the Boxers – an anti-Western militia – in the Boxers' siege of the foreign legations in Beijing.[33] An alliance of Britain, the United States, Japan, Russia, Germany, and France formed a 20,000-man army (the 15th Infantry Regiment made up a small part) and marched on Beijing to relieve the legations in August 1900.[34] The combined army quickly overpowered the Boxers and in September 1901 the

---

[30] Edward M. Coffman, "The American 15th Infantry Regiment in China, 1912-1938: A Vignette in Social History," *The Journal of Military History* 58, no. 1 (January, 1994): 58.

[31] Cornebise, *15th Infantry Regiment*, 21.

[32] Walter A. McDougall, *Promised Land, Crusader State: The American Encounter with the World Since 1776* (New York: Houghton Mifflin, 1997), 120-121; Cornebise, *15th Infantry Regiment*, 3, 27.

[33] Jonathan D. Spence, *The Search for Modern China* (New York: W.W. Norton & Company, 1990), 230-233.

[34] Diana Preston, *The Boxer Rebellion* (New York: Walker Publishing, 1999), 217-218. Cornebise, *15th Infantry Regiment,* 25. Eight countries actually contributed troops, but Italy and Austria-Hungary limited their contribution to naval elements.

alliance forced the Qing to sign the Boxer Protocols, an agreement that levied a crushing indemnity and allowed members of the alliance to station troops in the capital and along the line of communication from the capital to the coast.[35] But for ten years following the Boxer Rebellion, the United States government did not station troops in China and, in 1908, remitted payment of its portion of the indemnity.[36] These actions were characteristic of the American ambivalence towards imperialism and offered a marked contrast to other members of the alliance. The United States government wanted access to Chinese markets and a balance of foreign interests in China, but did not want to take part in foreign conquest – at least in the form of territorial concessions – or bear the costs associated with a large military contingent stationed in China.[37] This calculus became even more paradoxical after the fall of the Qing in 1912.

In the absence of a functioning Chinese government, the United States government feared that other foreign countries would attempt to expand their spheres of influence in China to the detriment of American interests and that pretenders to the vacated throne would threaten American citizens.[38] Despite these fears, the United States government still did not want to carve out American territory in China. When, at the behest of the State Department, the 15th Regiment came back to China in January 1912, the regiment, unlike its foreign counterparts who occupied

---

[35] Spence, *The Search*, 235.

[36] US Department of State, *United States Relations with China: Boxer Uprising to Cold War (1900-1949)*, US Government Printing Office, accessed April 1, 2014, http://2001-2009.state.gov/r/pa/ho/pubs/fs/90689.htm.

[37] Barbara W. Tuchman, *Stillwell and the American Experience in China, 1911-1945* (New York: Bantam Books, 1972), 19, 21, 38. Notably, the US did not have the same misgivings about exercising extraterritoriality which obviated Chinese jurisdiction in crimes committed by Americans in China. This, understandably, particularly upset many Chinese. Cornebise, *15th Infantry Regiment*, 24.

[38] Dennis L. Noble, *The Eagle and the Dragon: The United States Military in China, 1901-1937* (New York: Greenwood Press, 1990), 20-21.

territorial concessions, occupied bases leased from the putative Chinese government.[39] The

strange basing situation was further compounded by a confusing chain of command stemming

from a disagreement between the War Department and the State Department. Whereas the War

Department viewed a small force lacking a protected base as isolated and "increasingly exposed,"

the State Department thought a single regiment on leased land more than adequate to protect

American interests.[40] The War Department ceded the argument and the willingness to assign the

regiment its mission.[41] As a result, the tasks assigned by the State Department – keeping the

railway between Beijing and Tianjin open and protecting American citizens – became the de facto

mission for the regiment.[42] Marshall observed that while these arrangements may have made

sense in the context of China in 1912, by 1926, these arrangements, rife with "overlookings [*sic*],"

could "prove costly."[43]

The mission Marshall embraced as a lieutenant-colonel gave him first-hand experience

with the tension between the US government's principled position in China – a rejection of the

rapacious land grabs of imperialist powers – and its actual policy of maintaining access to

markets through the threat of force. Moreover, Marshall witnessed the tension between the US

military presence aimed at other outside powers as a hedge against attempts by these powers to

gain disproportionate economic advantages in China and the necessity to work with these powers

---

[39] Cornebise, *15th Infantry Regiment,* 41. This situation became even more confusing when American troops occupied a formerly German compound in 1917.

[40] Cornebise, 15th *Infantry Regiment,* 2.

[41] Noble, *The Eagle and the Dragon,* 22.

[42] Ibid., 34.

[43] Marshall, *PGCM vol. I,* 285-286. Marshall rejected the paternalistic and "fundamentally dismissive" Western characterizations of Chinese forces as "Celestial Opera Bouffe" easily defeated by "a few thousand disciplined and well-armed foreigners." Arthur Waldron, *From War to Nationalism: China's Turning Point, 1924-1925* (New York: Cambridge University Press, 1995), 54-55.

in times of crisis.[44] In both instances, he saw in stark outline the yawning divide between the aims of the United States government and the means to accomplish these aims. Shortly after his arrival, Marshall quickly realized that the composition and disposition of the regiment did not enable him to both protect "American citizens, business interests and missionaries and… keep open railway communication between Peking and the sea."[45]

Terrain and Troops Available

Tianjin's importance laid in its situation astride the confluence of rail the "leading port of the North China Plain."[46] In the 1920s, Tianjin sat forty miles inland from the mouth of Bohai Bay and connected Beijing (Peking) to the East China Sea via the Grand Canal and the Bei He (Pei Ho) River.[47] Southwest of Tianjin the Hai He (Hai Ho) River connected Tianjin to the Dagu (Taku) forts. These waterways were important both commercially and militarily as they allowed seafaring vessels access to the capital.[48] Tianjin also provided a critical rail nexus connecting the narrow Beijing-Shenyang corridor. This coastal corridor connected the massive alluvial plain that encompassed the lower reaches of the Yellow River to Manchuria – the region from whence the Qing Dynasty and Zhang Zuolin, a competitor for the throne, drew their power. Manchuria was otherwise separated by the low Yanshan mountain range (fig. 1).[49]

---

[44] Marshall, *PGCM vol. I*, 300.

[45] Cornebise, *15th Infantry Regiment*, 27.

[46] George B. Cressey, *China's Geographic Foundations* (New York: McGraw-Hill, 1934), 149; Spence, *The Search*, 250-251.

[47] Tianjin has grown from a city of nearly 1 million residents in 1920 to nearly 12 million today; what was a 40 mile gap between Tianjin and the bay has disappeared and the Tianjin metropolitan area extends all the way to the coast today.

[48] Cornebise, *15th Infantry Regiment*, 13.

[49] Spence, *The Search*, 251.

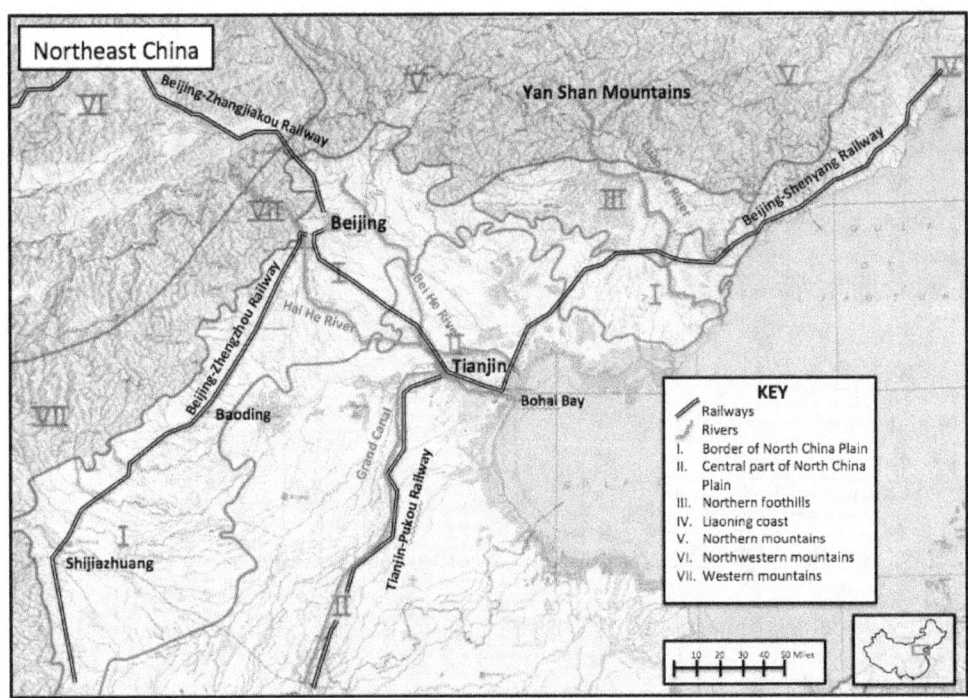

Figure 1. Northeast China

Sources: US Army Corps of Engineers, Strategic Intelligence Branch, *Hopeh-Shantung Region (China): Terrain Intelligence*. (Strategic engineering study, no. 150, Washington: US Army, 1945), 3. Highlighted railways traced from Jonathan Spence, *The Search*, 251.

When he arrived in 1924, Marshall had a total of approximately 750 men in Tianjin and a company outpost of about 100 men in Tangshan to ensure traffic on the Beijing-Shenyang (Peking-Mukden) railway.[50] Very shortly after his arrival, Marshall received an object lesson in the military importance of Tianjin when rail flow was halted between Tianjin and Shenyang as one Chinese warlord flowed his forces through the corridor.[51] Marshall also recognized that his paucity of American men and the expansive nature of his mission required extraordinary measures. When not actively engaged in protecting rail traffic or American lives, Marshall ensured rigorous field training and saw fit to institute a Chinese language program. He stated, "I

---

[50] Noble, *The Eagle and the Dragon*, 88, 90; Cornebise, *15th Infantry Regiment*, 12.

[51] Marshall, *PGCM vol. I*, 266.

think that the ability of every officer to speak Chinese, has saved us."[52] Marshall became very familiar with the ground between Tianjin, Tangshan, and Beijing, walking and riding hundreds of miles during his tour.[53]

Marshall understood that Tianjin's connection to the capital and trade drew the foreigners, who retained concessions in Tianjin, but its military value drew the warlords, who understood its importance in flowing troops from Manchuria or in stymying that same flow. The 15th Infantry Regiment's mission, then, required a deft hand to maneuver within a delicate and inordinately complex position with little guidance as to how to react in the face of large troop movements. Indeed, the War Department "placed much discretion in the hands of the commanding officer of the 15th."[54] Discretion was absolutely required, Marshall learned, because accomplishing the mission designated by the State Department by threat of force was impossible without a much larger contingent. Marshall stated in no uncertain terms that the best policy for foreigners, given their composition and disposition, would be "to avoid violent phases" through "sufficient tact and wisdom."[55] This Marshall would do in spades over his tour.

Enemy

China as a coherent state in the 1920s existed only as a confabulation: the last vestiges of dynastic empire, a system that had prevailed for millennia, had withered completely by 1912 when remnants of the Qing Dynasty disappeared into Manchuria.[56] Progressive Chinese

---

[52] Marshall, *PGCM vol. I*, 299.

[53] Ibid., 293.

[54] Cornebise, *15th Infantry Regiment*, 27.

[55] Marshall, *PGCM vol. I*, 294.

[56] Spence, *The Search*, 267.

politicians attempted to create a republic through national elections, but this solution collapsed under the weight of military strongmen vying for control of the capital. The inability of any of these strongmen to seize the Mandate of Heaven and unify the country left a gaping void into which flowed a cataract of warlord-controlled fiefdoms and competing ideologues.[57] In Northeast China and especially Beijing – a mere sixty-five miles away from the 15th Infantry Regiment's barracks – a succession of warlords backed by large armies and foreign powers took turns controlling the nominal seat of Chinese power. By 1924, three factions vied for control.

The intrigue and fighting between the armies of Feng Yuxiang (Feng Yu-hsiang), Wu Peifu (Wu Pei-fu), and Zhang Zuolin (Chang Tso-lin) reads like Shakespearean tragedy.[58] Attempts to consolidate power by one faction or another generated temporary alliances among opponents, concomitant coups d'état, and brief seasonal wars in which no faction gained a decisive advantage. Between 1916 and 1927, military control of the area between Beijing and Tianjin (which did not, in this period, guarantee control of anything beyond this area) changed hands no fewer than four times.[59] In an attempt to understand the situation in the summer of 1924, Brigadier General William Connor, Commander of American Forces in China, visited the headquarters of all three factions. Of Marshal Wu Peifu's forces – numbering over one hundred thousand in total – Connor wrote, "my impression of the soldiers… was more favorable than that

---

[57] Spence, *The Search,* 271, 276, 334.

[58] Spence, *The Search,* 288-290, 341-342; Cornebise, *15th Infantry Regiment,* 32-33. As Premier of China in 1916 by virtue of being Yuan Shikai's designated successor, Duan Qirui probably had the most legitimate claim to rule of the republic. This argument was lost, of course, on the opposing warlords.

[59] Spence, *The Search,* 341, 363-364; Cornebise, *15th Infantry Regiment,* 32-33. This includes the following wars: Zhili-Anhui War in July of 1920, in which Zhang Zuolin took control of Beijing; the First Zhili-Fengtian War in the spring of 1922, in which Wu Peifu took control of the central government, the Second Zhili-Fengtian War in the autumn of 1924, which Feng Yuxiang supposedly won, but which only allowed him to make common cause with Zhang Zuolin and reinstall Duan Qirui as prime minister (Duan had served in this capacity after Yuan Shikai's death in 1916), and finally the Guominjun-Fengtian War in November of 1925 to April of 1926 which saw the ouster of Feng Yuxiang and the reemergence of the Zhang Zuolin – Wu Peifu alliance until both were defeated during the Northern Expedition in 1928.

produced by any other Chinese soldiers that I have seen."[60] Connor also lauded Wu's ability to "instill confidence in his officers and men." Yet Connor qualified his assessment by questioning Wu's ability to secure the loyalty of his most senior generals.[61] Given the predilection for intrigue among senior Chinese generals (Wu himself had aligned with both Feng Yuxiang and Zhang Zuolin at different times), Connor's caveat speaks volumes. Lieutenant Colonel George Marshall's view on the situation was more direct: "No one ventures to predict just what is to happen. Chinese methods are too devious for foreign penetration."[62] The situation in China was both fluid and violent; large and capable armies wielded by ambitious men routinely clashed within miles of the 15th Infantry Regiment.

Marshall believed that on arrival to the 15th Infantry Regiment he would become the executive officer (XO), but the previous commander, Colonel Campbell King, departed in July, 1924 and his replacement, Colonel William K. Naylor, would not arrive until November 22, 1924.[63] Coincidentally, in that window and only just after Marshall's arrival in China, Zhang Zuolin and the Fengtian Army in Manchuria decided to make common cause with Sun Yat-sen in the south and depose the warlords in control of Beijing: Wu Peifu and Feng Yuxiang.[64] By mid-October, Wu Peifu appeared ready to seize the initiative after having successfully blocked

---

[60] BG William D. Connor, to Adjutant General and G-2 Division, War Department, General Staff United States Army, "Notes on visit to Marshal Wu Pei Fu's Headquarters," June 4, 1924, Reel 5, Document 0325 in *China, 1911-1941 [microfilm]: U.S. Military Intelligence Reports*, United States War Department, Military Intelligence Division, eds. Paul Kesaris and Lester, Robert, 1983.

[61] Ibid.

[62] Marshall, *PGCM vol I*, 266. He wrote this in September of 1924 in a letter to MG John L. Hines.

[63] Ibid., 264, Cornebise, *15th Infantry Regiment,* 62.

[64] Sun Yat-sen is rendered Sun Zhongshang in *pinyin*. I chose Yat-sen as this is more widely known.

Zhang's advance along the axis of advance in the Beijing-Shenyang corridor. As Wu prepared to personally lead the attack into Manchuria, his putative ally and subordinate Feng Yuxiang (directed by Wu Peifu to protect Beijing), deposed the president in Beijing and declared common cause with Zhang Zuolin. As a result, Wu Peifu faced potential encirclement and annihilation. Instead, he and some 2,000 men embarked on frigates and sailed to central China.[65] Tianjin was a focal point during this fight – the so-called Second Fengtian-Zhili War – and Marshall had to ensure that the 100,000 troops that flowed through Tianjin either to or from the fighting fronts did not attack the foreign concessions (fig. 2). He also had to ensure that his troops did not aggravate the situation with unnecessary violence. On top of these delicate tasks, Marshall was also supposed to ensure that the confrontation between warlords did not interdict international rail traffic from Beijing to Tianjin.[66] Despite an inability to keep the rails completely clear, Marshall performed these duties well enough to receive a commendation from BG Connor who cited his "unusual tact, patience, and foresight" in dealing with the opposed forces.[67]

---

[65] Waldron, *From War*, 186-187.

[66] Marshall, *PGCM vol. I*, 270-271.

[67] Ibid., 270.

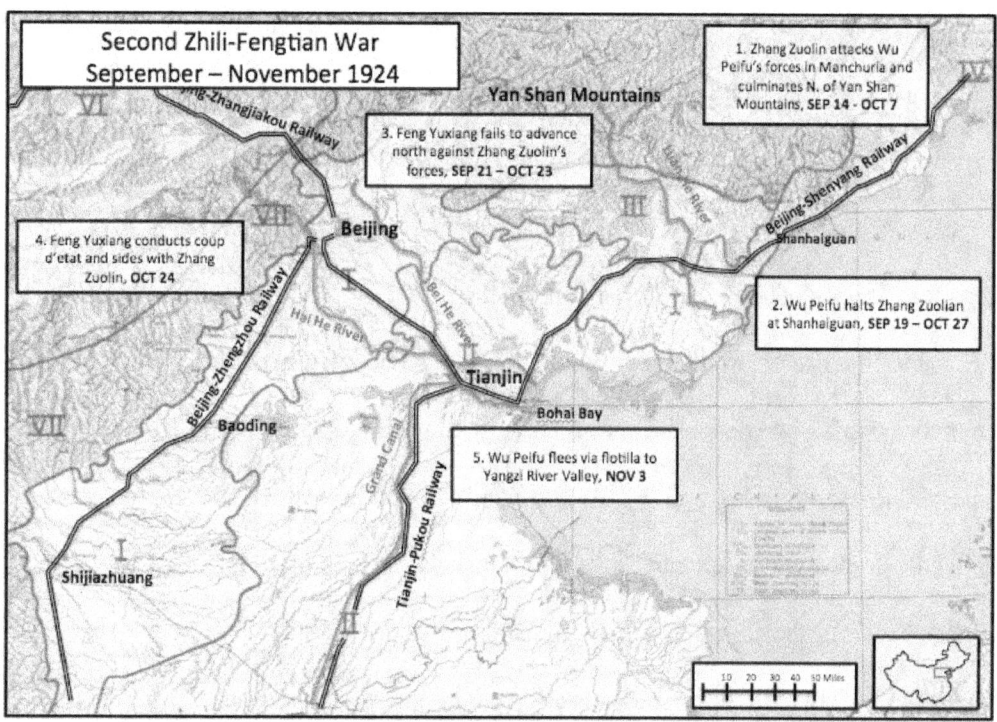

Figure 2. Second Zhili-Fengtian War

Sources: US Army Corps of Engineers, *Hopeh-Shantung Region (China): Terrain Intelligence*, 3. Content from Arthur Waldron, *From War to Nationalism: China's Turning Point, 1924-1925* (New York: Cambridge University Press, 1995), 73.

This situation virtually repeated itself in December 1925. Colonel Naylor, the regimental commander, was ill and LTC Marshall again took command.[68] This series of battles – the so-called Guominjun-Fengtian War – witnessed the same warlords fighting in a different configuration: this time with Feng Yuxiang the odd man out. Tianjin was again a focus for the competing armies and Marshall, once more, was able to prevent an exchange of hostilities between his troops and the Chinese forces despite having the tasks of securing foreign rail traffic and preventing the Chinese investment of the foreign concessions or the American compound. In one instance, Marshall, backed by a single platoon, demanded that a Chinese regiment evacuate a

---

[68] Marshall, *PGCM vol. I*, 284.

police headquarters in use by the 15th Infantry Regiment.[69] Marshall by this time spoke some Chinese. He was able to secure the police headquarters by virtue of demanding disarmament if they stayed and by "a touch of Chinese polite formality in expression."[70] Marshall's close interaction with the Chinese during these incidents gave him keen insight into how the Chinese forces fought each other on the ground and in the palace.

Intelligence reports at the time also provided a detailed depiction of the broader maneuvers. Sitting astride a critical rail juncture allowed the 15th Infantry Regiment's intelligence officer to monitor the use of rail by the combatants to move troops and equipment. As one report notes, "due to the unusual number of troop trains and the lack of cooperation between the various military leaders… the whole system would soon be so congested that ordinary traffic would be impossible."[71] Also, when the warlords allowed the international trains to run, the trains passed through contested areas unmolested and "had the opportunity of witnessing more of the civil war than any others…"[72] Coupled with Tianjin's location along a major axis of advance, Marshall could assess everything from the use of rail –"they misuse [it] terribly" – to the character of the individual fighting man: "a Chinese soldier will go farther on a dough ball than an American soldier on a full ration and his Y.M.C.A. or Red Cross 'hot chocolate.'"[73]

Marshall also witnessed some of the fighting in the Second Fengtian-Zhili and the Guominjun-Fengtian Wars first-hand. For Marshall, veteran of industrialized warfare in Europe, the combination of air bombing, artillery, trench warfare and attempts to maneuver enormous

---

[69] Cornebise, *15th Infantry Regiment*, 40.

[70] Ibid., Marshall, *PGCM vol. I*, 299, 294.

[71] Captain Walter C. Phillips, "Memo: Allied Trains during Chili-Fengtien 1924 War," January 17, 1925, Reel 5, Document 509 in *China, 1911-1941 [microfilm]: U.S. Military Intelligence Reports*, United States War Department, Military Intelligence Division, eds. Paul Kesaris and Lester, Robert, 1983.

[72] Marshall, *PGCM vol. I*, 268.

[73] Ibid., 272.

forces by the opposing sides "smack[ed] much the old war time atmosphere."[74] Indeed, when Wu

Peifu's army of 120,000 men halted Zhang Zuolin in 1924 along the Tianjin-Shenyang corridor, it

did so at the cost of some 10,000 casualties.[75] Though the machinations in Beijing may have

seemed altogether foreign to Marshall, the attempt to smash through stalemates and the resulting

steady "streams of horribly wounded casualties" were all too familiar.[76] Some of the lessons

drawn from these brief conflicts became themes in his correspondence over the three-year tour;

two decades later these lessons would come to the fore.

Civilian Considerations and Time

The lesson that appears most frequently in Marshall's correspondence concerns the

inability of the foreign contingent (himself included) to understand the Chinese political

environment.[77] Marshall had little difficulty in estimating the military efficacy of the various

fighting factions, but the political situation was "the most interesting problem in the world today,

and the most dangerous."[78] Intelligence produced at the time by the 15th Infantry Regiment

described the various political actors involved – civilian and military, but could not clarify

relationships beyond the very basic interactions of various figureheads and generals.[79] Marshall

---

[74] Marshall, *PGCM vol. I*, 266.

[75] Waldron, *From War*, 104, 113.

[76] Ibid., 71.

[77] Marshall, *PGCM vol. I*, 275, 282, 293, 294, 295, 299, 300.

[78] Ibid., 272, 299.

[79] Captain Walter C. Phillips "Situation Survey for the Period of October 18th to December 31st 1924: Chihli-Fengtien War," January 30, 1925, Reel 7, Document 0824 in *China, 1911-1941 [microfilm]: U.S. Military Intelligence Reports*, United States War Department, Military Intelligence Division, eds. Paul Kesaris and Lester, Robert, 1983. The 15th Infantry Regiment commander was on the distribution list for these reports indicating that Marshall would have had full knowledge of the contents.

expressed frustration with this lack of knowledge; late in his tour with the 15th he stated, "how the Powers should deal with China is a question almost impossible to answer."[80]

The inscrutability of the political situation informed Marshall's understanding of the fragility of the American government's military position in China. BG Connor explained this situation in a secret memo to the American minister to China after the crisis in December 1925.[81] Connor pointed out that the increasingly capable armies and the spread of incipient nationalism had fundamentally changed the environment and that when "our bluff was called" regarding the willingness to expend American blood to keep the international trains open in 1924 and 1925, the Americans and other foreign contingents were forced to back down.[82] The delicate nature of the American position – again, the regiment leased its bases from China – heightened the dangers associated with the spread of nationalism and xenophobic sentiment in China. None of this was lost on Marshall who recognized that Chinese nationalism could quickly bloom into "violent and unreasoning outbreaks."[83]

Marshall's frustration with Chinese politics also stemmed from the speed with which inscrutable palace machinations could fundamentally change the course of military events on the ground. Marshall knew quite well the importance of key terrain to the movement of large units and he understood even better the importance of Tianjin as key terrain. But the situation on the ground in Tianjin could and did completely change because of civilian and military political maneuvers in Beijing. This frustrating situation and "interesting problem" did not prevent Marshall from making an assessment as to its remedy.

---

[80] Marshall, *PGCM vol. I*, 294.

[81] Cornebise, *15th Infantry Regiment*, 40.

[82] Ibid., 41.

[83] Marshall, *PGCM vol. I*, 294.

Marshall noted that the Chinese commander who "best addressed the basic needs of the populace and of the average soldier, commanded not only the most loyalty, but the best soldiers."[84] As Marshall saw it, the key to control of China lay in a leader who could harness nationalism and xenophobia, meet the needs of the populace, and navigate the political tidewaters of Beijing. Marshall wrote in January 1925, "a strong man combining the qualities of statesman, politician and military chief, can build up an army in China that would make foreign influence an extremely difficult, if not perilous affair inland."[85] Shortly after Marshall wrote this letter, Sun Yat-sen's successor, Chiang Kai-shek, worked to consolidate power in southern China; two years later, Chiang began the Northern Expedition to consolidate China and end the rule of warlords.[86]

By the end of Marshall's first stay in China, the pace of change in the operational environment had quickened. When he arrived in September 1924, the US State Department, even if it repudiated the imperialistic undertones of the implicit threat of force, still believed a single regiment capable of accomplishing the American mission in China. But by the end of 1925, the tenuous nature of the American military presence had become much clearer; without at least tacit consent from the Chinese, the regiment could not accomplish its mission. Only the continued consent obviated the need for the US government to decide between abandoning China and reinforcing the 15th Infantry Regiment.

When Marshall departed in May 1927, Chiang Kai-shek, embodying at least in part the strong man Marshall envisaged, had cobbled together "as many dissident elements as possible" to defeat the warlords vying for Beijing.[87] By 1928, Chiang succeeded in unifying China, even if he

---

[84] Cornebise, *15th Infantry Regiment*, 35.

[85] Marshall, *PGCM vol. I*, 271.

[86] Spence, *The Search*, 344; Donald A. Jordan, *The Northern Expedition: China's national Revolution of 1926-1928* (Honolulu: The University Press of Hawaii, 1976), 68. I employ Chiang Kai-shek instead of the *pinyin* Jiang Jieshi because of the familiarity of the former Romanization.

[87] Marshall, *PGCM vol. I*, 304; Jordan, *The Northern Expedition*, x.

had not succeeded in centralizing his authority in a single government.[88] This latter defect would, of course, require Marshall's second tour in China twenty years later.

Marshall's three years of service with the 15th Infantry Regiment included command of the 15th "during two of the most crucial periods of its history in China."[89] These crucial periods gave Marshall insight into the extent of military and political influence of foreign countries and foreigners in China. He learned that the size of China coupled with the complex nature of the political and military environments limited the influence of foreigners and the employment of military power on anything less than a massive scale. Marshall also gleaned critical lessons about the Chinese way of warfare – specifically about the character of Chinese soldiers and their relationship with the Chinese populace.[90] These lessons laid fallow for twenty years, but, during and especially after World War II, sprang to life as Marshall was called once again to exercise tact and patience in China.

Section Two: Nanjing, Chongqing, and Lessons Applied, 1946-1947

When General Marshall landed in Shanghai on December 20, 1945, much had changed for both Marshall and China.[91] In the two decades since leaving China, Marshall's aperture widened from a single regiment to the entire American army. As the US Army chief of staff from July 1937 to November 1945, Marshall shepherded the US Army through its expansion,

---

[88] Jordan, *The Northern Expedition*, 295.

[89] Cornebise, *15th Infantry Regiment*, 77.

[90] Michael A. Bonura, *Under the Shadow of Napoleon: French Influence on the American Way of Warfare from the War of 1812 to the Outbreak of WWII* (New York: New York University Press, 2012), 3. The citation describes a "way of warfare" for any country as its acceptable types of soldiers, armies, practices, and traditions.

[91] John Hart Caughey, *The Marshall Mission to China, 1945-1947: The Letters and Diary of Colonel John Hart Caughey,* ed. Roger B. Jeans (Lanham, MD: Rowman & Littlefield Publishers, Inc., 2011), xix.

participation, and victory in World War II.[92] In a ceremony celebrating Marshall's brief retirement on November 26, 1945, President Truman stated, "in a war unparalleled in magnitude and in horror, millions of Americans gave their country outstanding service. General of the Army George C. Marshall gave it victory."[93]

Change for China was less sanguine. For the decade following Marshall's departure, Chiang Kai-shek struggled to consolidate power.[94] By 1937, instead of enacting desperately needed political or social reforms or providing a coherent response to the menacing Japanese presence in Manchuria, Chiang Kai-shek doggedly focused on the extermination of an intractable communist insurgency led by Mao Zedong.[95] As a result, the Nationalist government was unprepared for Japan's full-scale invasion and occupation of China's key industrial and agricultural centers in July 1937. Chiang and Mao temporarily set aside their differences and resisted the Japanese occupation for the next seven years, longer than any other country invaded by Japan.[96]

The Chinese struggle against the Japanese, aided by the United States, succeeded in tying a million Japanese troops to the Chinese mainland. While this success enabled the Allied advance across the Pacific, it came at an enormous cost: millions of Chinese lives lost, millions more displaced, a shattered economy and a "tired, corrupt and deteriorating" Nationalist government.[97] Japanese capitulation in July 1945, rather than coalesce the Chinese Communists and Nationalists

---

[92] Marshall, *Marshall Interviews*, x-xi.

[93] Pogue, *Marshall: Statesman*, 1.

[94] Spence, *The Search*, 399-402.

[95] Barbara W. Tuchman, *Stillwell and the American Experience in China, 1911-1945* (New York: Bantam Books, 1972), 166.

[96] Spence, *The Search*, 437. Tuchman, *Stillwell*, 2. Marshall maintained awareness of the situation in China during this period via Generals Stillwell and Wedemeyer, with whom he maintained contact. Marshall, *PGCM vol III*, 275, 335-336.

[97] Tuchman, *Stillwell*, 2-3.

who had fought a common enemy for so long, left them competing to fill the vacuum.[98] The

Soviet Union's tentative moves towards making common cause with the CCP presented the US

government with the familiar dilemma of trying to balance foreign interests in China with its own

national interests while respecting, or at least acknowledging, Chinese autonomy.[99] In December

1945 when President Truman appointed General Marshall to mediate a peace between the CCP

and GMD, the stakes were enormous: without peace, China could neither aid in enforcing the

Japanese surrender nor could it act as a potential balance to the Soviet Union's presence. Indeed,

when Marshall accepted Truman's mission, the hard-fought Pacific victory lurched towards

disintegration.[100] This section examines Marshall's attempt to meet the President's intent in terms

of mission, troops, terrain, time, enemy, and civilian considerations. Again, the mission variables

condense Marshall's thinking and provide a structure for comparison to the lessons he learned in

the 1920s.

Mission

Marshall was retired for all of twenty-four hours when he received the call from President

Truman asking him to go to China.[101] Patrick Hurley, the previous ambassador to China,

surprised the President when he resigned on 27 November – the day after Marshall's retirement.

---

[98] Odd Arne Westad, *Decisive Encounters: The Chinese Civil War, 1946-1950* (Stanford: Stanford University Press, 2003), 7.

[99] Westad, *Decisive Encounters*, 31.

[100] US Department of State, Office of Far Eastern Affairs, *Foreign Relations of the United States, 1945, vol. 7*, "The Marshall Mission: Instructions to General of the Army George C. Marshall Regarding United States Policy Towards China: First Conferences in China (1945), US Government Printing Office," accessed March 24, 2014, http://digital.library.wisc.edu/1711. dl/FRUS.FRUS1945v07 (), 747, hereafter cited as *FRUS, 1945, vol. 7*; Marshall, *PGCM vol. V*, 396, 402, 481. Balancing the interests of the Soviet Union was not a stated aim in President Truman's instructions to Marshall as the USSR was still allied to the United States government, but "balancing" was discussed in other documents, mostly referencing an Open Door policy in Manchuria.

[101] Marshall, *PGCM vol. V*, 372.

Hurley resigned because of what he termed "the wide discrepancy between our announced policies and our conduct of international relations."[102] Marshall, more familiar with such discrepancies – even if he disagreed with the particulars of Hurley's assessment – received the appointment because of the magnitude of the problems in China and because the President "had great reverence for the Chief of Staff and he believed General Marshall could do no wrong."[103] Along with the President's trust and confidence, Marshall received an explicit and publicly aired set of instructions from the President.[104] President Truman directed Marshall to form a representative consultative conference as a first step towards a unified government, to bring about a cessation of hostilities, and to evacuate Japanese troops from China.[105] Truman also included a top-secret proviso that, in Marshall's words, placed Marshall "on the horns of a dilemma."[106]

The secret proviso concerned the position of the United States government vis-à-vis Chiang Kai-shek and the Nationalists should Marshall fail to bring the competing parties to the table. Marshall wanted explicit clarification as to whether Truman would authorize him to risk the President's political capital. In a meeting with the President on 14 December, Marshall stated to the President that he believed Truman's intent "was that in the event that I was unable to secure the necessary action by the Generalissimo [Chiang Kai-shek], it would still be necessary for the

---

[102] US Department of State, *The China White Paper, August 1949* (Stanford: Stanford University Press, 1967), 581.

[103] Mathew J. Connelly, Oral History Interview conducted August 21, 1968, Harry S. Truman Library Website, accessed September 1, 2014, http://www.trumanlibrary.org/oralhist/connly3.htm, 359.

[104] Hurley believed that the career China men in the Foreign Service actively opposed American policy by siding with Chinese Communists. Ibid., 582-583. Marshall did not seem to share his opinion and worked well with the China experts. Marshall, *PGCM vol. V*, 413-415.

[105] US Department of State, *FRUS, 1945, vol. 7*, 755-757; Larry I. Bland, ed. *George C. Marshall's Mediation Mission to China* (Lexington, VA: George C. Marshall Research Foundation, 1998), 555. Bland notes that Marshall worked closely with the State Department to formulate the instructions issued to him by Truman.

[106] Marshall, *PGCM vol. V*, 374.

U.S. government, through me, to continue to back... the Generalissimo..."[107] The President confirmed this and added that "he would back me in my decisions, that he had confidence in my judgment."[108] Truman's clarification had two effects. First, the President created a dilemma: Marshall would have to broker a settlement between Chiang and Mao while simultaneously backing Chiang and the GMD.[109] This sort of diplomacy, which had bested Hurley, required a highly discrete and deft hand. Second, the President gave Marshall incredible latitude to achieve the strategic objective of a stable China. If Marshall deemed compromise impossible, then he could, vested with plenipotentiary power, buttress the Nationalists as he saw fit to accomplish the objective of peace in China. The possibilities afforded by this latitude became more distinct as Marshall evaluated the situation in China at the end of 1945.

Time and Troops Available

Upon receiving his instructions from the President, George Marshall knew immediately that his ability to accomplish his mission hinged on time.[110] He needed time to bring the opposing parties to the negotiating table, time to implement a cease-fire, and time to establish a framework for a unified military and government. He knew that every delay to the start of negotiations risked intractability between the opposed parties; as the fighting spread further afield, especially if it involved the Soviets, the ability to bring the violence to heel decreased.[111] Beyond this risk,

---

[107] Marshall, *PGCM vol. V*, 393.

[108] Ibid.

[109] Caughey, *The Marshall Mission*, 1.

[110] Marshall, *PGCM vol. V*, 374. In this top secret memorandum sent to Admiral William Leahy on November, 30, 1945, Marshall noted the criticality of minimizing delays in the negotiations. Admiral Leahy served as the Chief of Staff to the Commander in Chief, a position created by Franklin D. Roosevelt to act in the same capacity as the Chairman of the Joint Chiefs of Staff does today.

[111] Marshall, *PGCM vol. V*, 374.

Marshall saw another factor that limited the time he had to jumpstart negotiations: the presence of the Japanese.

The President's third directive to Marshall – evacuate the Japanese from China – stemmed from the fear that a large, armed Japanese force in China, even if officially surrendered, could "hold the balance of power in certain areas" or that it could be employed by one faction or the other to exacerbate the civil war.[112] Either of these scenarios risked not just peace in China but peace in the region as well. Therefore "the orderly and rapid deportation of the Japanese" was Marshall's first priority.[113] This priority was complicated by the relatively small American troop presence in China and the fact that neither the Chinese nor the Japanese had the capacity to move the surrendered forces back to Japan.[114] By December 1946, Marshall had two US Marine divisions and approximately one hundred landing craft at his disposal.[115] Though capable of transporting the surrendered Japanese, this small contingent could not secure even a fraction of the materiel or facilities held by the Japanese in North China and Manchuria.[116] The US government, unwilling to cede these facilities or materiel to Russian or Chinese Communists, would have to rely on Chiang Kai-shek's troops, but the GMD troops would require American transport from South China.[117] Herein lay the bind: Marshall needed to appear as an honest broker to bring both sides to the table, but the clock was ticking to remove the Japanese. At the same

---

[112] Marshall, *PGCM vol. V*, 383.

[113] Ibid.

[114] Ibid.

[115] Marshall, *PGCM vol. V*, 374n3, 375; Wang Chen-main, "Marshall's Approaches to the Mediation Effort," in *George C. Marshall's Mediation Mission to China,* ed. Larry I Bland (Lexington, VA: George C. Marshall Research Foundation, 1998), 23. These approximately 53,000 troops were located these troops and transports were located at the critical port cities in North China including Tianjin.

[116] Caughey, *The Marshall Mission,* 10. Estimates for Japanese requiring repatriation were 2.15 million Japanese soldiers and more than 1.75 million Japanese civilians.

[117] Marshall, *PGCM vol. V*, 383.

time, replacing the Japanese with GMD forces would appear to favor Chiang Kai-shek and could thwart negotiations before they started. Marshall's solution relied on his deft hand and an understanding of the opposed parties.

To avoid prejudicing either the CCP or the GMD, Marshall decided to make all American preparations for logistical support to move the GMD into Japanese positions secret and "to utilize that uncertainty for the purpose of bringing influence to bear" on both parties.[118] Marshall would tell Chiang Kai-shek that unless he negotiated a settlement with the Communists, the US military would not move his troops to take possession of the Japanese holdings and would hold all support in abeyance. Marshall would alternately tell the CCP that without their willingness to negotiate, he would support the GMD movement north.[119]

The plan was risky: if Chiang refused to negotiate, Marshall would still need to employ American assets to move GMD troops to take possession of Japanese installations. His leverage with both the GMD and the CCP could evaporate before the parties even sat down to negotiate.[120] Marshall sought to mitigate this by risk communicating his delicate position in person. On December 14, 1945, a week prior to leaving for China, he directed that "no negotiations would be conducted with Chinese officials without a clearance" from Marshall.[121] Additionally, Marshall knew that his ability to bring the parties to the table would depend on their relative position on the

---

[118] Marshall, *PGCM vol. V*, 385.

[119] Ibid.

[120] Marshall, *PGCM vol. V*, 386, 393; Wang Chen-main, "Marshall's Approaches to the Mediation Effort," in *George C. Marshall's Mediation Mission to China,* ed. Larry I Bland (Lexington, VA: George C. Marshall Research Foundation, 1998), 23.

[121] Marshall, *PGCM vol. V*, 395.

battlefield. Though time was Marshall's most precious commodity, he would have to assess for himself the ground and the state of the forces in opposition.[122]

Enemy and Terrain

Marshall worked quickly to evaluate the opposed forces and bring them to the negotiation table in as "inobtrusive" a manner as possible.[123] On 10 January, Marshall wrote to Truman that he had achieved the cease-fire. He also reported that Zhou Enlai (Chou En-lai), the CCP representative, and Chiang Kai-shek both asked Marshall to develop and administer the plan to reorganize China's army.[124] By the end of January, Colonel John Caughey, Marshall's executive officer during the mission, noted that Marshall was "about ten jumps further ahead than everybody else… He has got his finger on things particularly China, and what makes China tick."[125] Marshall's understanding and initial successes resulted from frequent trips between Chongqing (Chunking), the provisional capital and preferred location for Zhou Enlai, and Nanjing (Nanking), the Nationalist Capital and home to Chiang Kai-shek. Between 20 December 1945 and 10 January 1946, Marshall conducted at least thirty-five formal meetings, conferences, or negotiations with leaders of the CCP and GMD.[126] For Marshall, this was time well spent; he

---

[122] Marshall, *PGCM vol. V*, 391. In a letter to a friend prior to his departure to China, Marshall wrote that the preparatory materials about the fighting in China from the State and War Department, though engrossing, were "very superficial."

[123] Marshall, *PGCM vol. V*, 444. In other letters to Truman, Marshall reiterates the point that he does not want to dictate terms to the combatants, but that they must come to the position of their own accord. Marshall, *PGCM vol. V*, 428.

[124] Marshall, *PGCM vol. V*, 416-417.

[125] Caughey, *The Marshall Mission*, 74. COL Caughey became Marshall's executive officer on January 1 after being transferred from Lieutenant General Albert C. Wedemeyer's (Commanding General of the China Theater) staff on which he had served since November 1944. Wedemeyer called Caughey one of his "ablest officers." Caughey, *The Marshall Mission*, 9.

[126] General Marshall's Daily Appointments 27 November 1945 – 21 January 1947, in *George C. Marshall's Mediation Mission to China*, ed. Larry I Bland (Lexington, VA: George C. Marshall Research Foundation, 1998), 596-598. Marshall also met with the so-called "Third Party"

gained insight into the leadership, capabilities, and limitations of the Communists and Nationalists.

The Communists surprised Marshall. He assumed prior to leaving for China that the Communists would "block all progress in negotiations... as the delay [was] to their advantage," but found them "more responsive to the dictates" of the negotiation committee.[127] Marshall noted that this responsiveness likely stemmed from the Communists' "tightly held organization, whereas on the Nationalist side there were many contentious elements."[128] Marshall, seeking an informational advantage in negotiations, also requested and received ULTRA code-breakers who quickly discerned differences in what Chiang Kai-shek agreed to in negotiations and the orders he issued to his commanders in the field.[129] Chiang's machinations both buttressed Marshall's assessment of the Nationalists' lack of cohesion and signaled the beginning of his frustration with Chiang's opaque political maneuvers.

Additional insight into the potential efficacy of the cease-fire came in the seventy-two hours between its signing on 10 January and its implementation on midnight of 13 January. In this short period, violence spiked in the most contested areas of northern China as each side maneuvered to gain positional advantage before the cease-fire went into effect.[130] Marshall anticipated this violence and knew that without an effective mechanism to ensure compliance to

---

representatives like the Democratic League. While Marshall saw potential in these groups, they would not impact the final outcome of the Mission. Yuemei Sun, "The Third Force in the Marshall Mission," Master's thesis (University of Georgia, 2000), 1-3.

[127] Marshall, *PGCM vol. V*, 374; George C. Marshall, "Memorandum for Harry S. Truman on the China Mission, 17 May 1954," in *George C. Marshall's Mediation Mission to China,* ed. Larry I Bland (Lexington, VA: George C. Marshall Research Foundation, 1998), 562.

[128] Marshall, "Memorandum for Harry S. Truman," 562.

[129] Marshall, *PGCM vol. V*, 420n2.

[130] US Department of State, Office of Far Eastern Affairs, *Foreign Relations of the United States [FRUS], 1946, vol. 9. The Far East: China,* US Government Printing Office, accessed August 5, 2014, http://digital.library.wisc.edu/1711.dl/FRUS.FRUS1946v09, 345-347.

the cease-fire, violence and reprisals would likely continue.[131] The agreed upon monitoring

mechanism consisted of "truce teams" made up of a combination of American, Communist, and

Nationalist officers with interpreters who would monitor and adjudicate potential violations.[132]

Though these teams began traveling to units near the contested terrain immediately after the

feuding parties signed the cease-fire, sporadic violence continued until the end of February when

the cease-fire and the efforts of the teams secured a tense peace.[133] Marshall believed that this

peace could only last if the militaries from both sides demobilized the majority of their forces and

unified the rest as quickly as possible.[134] To that end, he wanted to tour "the most troubled areas"

himself; in the first week of March, he flew to the most contested areas in northern China.[135] His

conclusions only confirmed the importance of time and the need for a political solution.

Marshall came away from this trip with an even clearer depiction of the battlefield.

Though the Nationalists had nearly three times as many men as the Communists, the Nationalists

controlled the cities but had very little control over their lines of communication (fig. 3).[136] This

same pattern of composition and disposition appeared again over the next three months in

Manchuria. Neither the CCP nor the GMD believed the cease-fire agreed to in January

encompassed Manchuria, and as the Soviet Union withdrew from Manchuria, both sides looked

to fill the vacuum.[137] The Communists had a distinct advantage as the Soviets timed their

---

[131] Marshall, *PGCM vol. V*, 417n1.

[132] Marshall, *PGCM vol. V*, 421.

[133] Andrew Birtle, "The Marshall Mission: A Peacekeeping Mission that Failed," *Military Review* 80, iss. 2 (March/April 2000): 100.

[134] Marshall, *PGCM vol. V*, 459.

[135] Marshall, *PGCM vol. V*, 459; General Marshall's Daily Appointments, 600-601.

[136] Marshall, *PGCM vol. V*, 419n2, 421-422. The Nationalists had an estimated 3.14 million men versus the Communists 1.2 million.

[137] Birtle, "A Peacekeeping Mission that Failed," 101.

withdrawals with CCP movements into Manchuria.[138] Despite this advantage, Chiang Kai-shek

seized Siping in May and demanded the Communists cede the larger Manchurian city of

Changchun.[139] These maneuvers required another massive effort by Marshall to bring about a

second cease-fire, this one specifically for Manchuria, which he secured in June.[140] Again, though,

Chiang Kai-shek placed himself in a position of control over a few cities, in an area surrounded

by Communists and with tenuous control of his increasingly long lines of communication. To

Marshall, these efforts seemed particularly fraught given the view of the Nationalist Government

in the eyes of many Chinese.

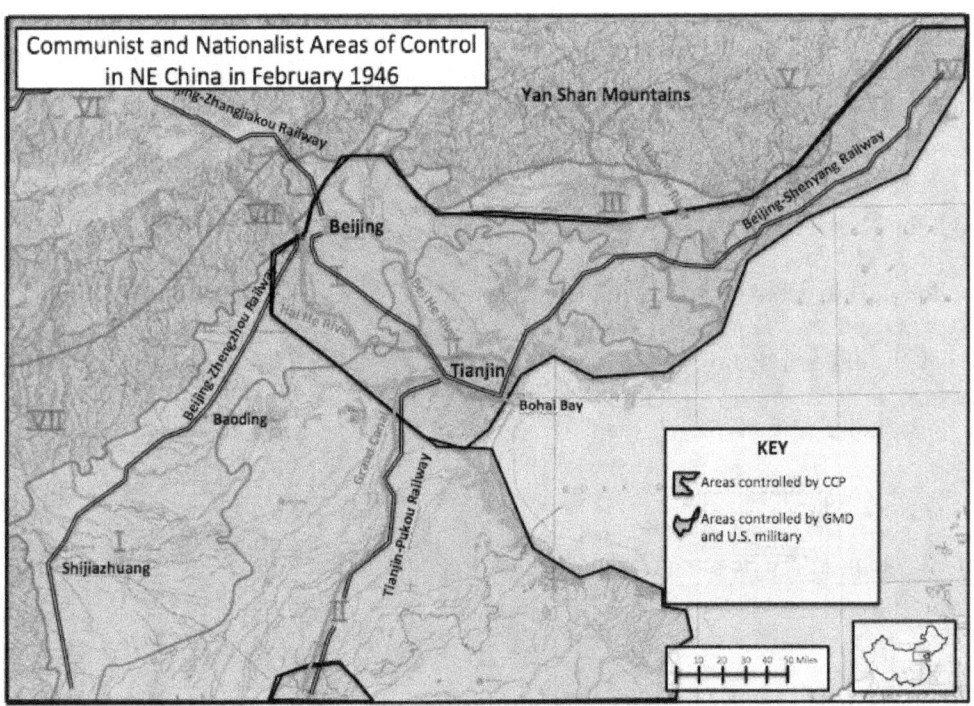

Figure 3. Communist and Nationalist Areas of Control

Sources. US Army Corps of Engineers, *Hopeh-Shantung Region (China): Terrain Intelligence*, 3. Content from Marshall, PGCM vol. V, 487.

---

[138] Spence, *The Search*, 494-495.

[139] Marshall, *PGCM vol. V*, 553.

[140] Birtle, "A Peacekeeping Mission that Failed," 101.

Civilian Considerations

From the outset of his mission, Marshall attempted to obtain as much information as he could, "particularly the opinions of people in all walks of life."[141] What he found only intensified his efforts to form a unified government: Marshall wrote that "the majority" of the civilians with whom he met "were bitterly hostile to [the Nationalist] Government."[142] Early in his mission, Marshall wrote to Truman of an incident of "starved people clamoring for supplies… and… for justice against puppet officials they accused of murder, brutality and rapine" in a Government controlled area.[143] Even after the June cease-fire, Chiang Kai-shek's priority seemed to mirror to his priority in 1937: an obdurate resolve towards destruction of the Communists. In a meeting between Marshall and Chiang on 29 June, Marshall told Chiang that the Nationalists "would be judged by the world… as having unnecessarily plunged the country into chaos by implacable demands and the evident desire to pursue a policy of military settlement."[144]

General Marshall made several more attempts to bring the Communists and Nationalists to accord, but by early September 1946, he did not attempt to halt the reduction of American forces and on 7 January 1947 stated publicly that he could not reconcile the opposed parties.[145] Marshall noted in his statement on 7 January that, "though I speak as a soldier, I must here also deplore the dominating influence of the military. Their dominance accentuates the weakness of civil government in China."[146] Marshall knew that Chiang's continued insistence on the destruction of the Communists could never lend itself to peace.

---

[141] Marshall, "Memorandum for Harry S. Truman," 560.

[142] Marshall, "Memorandum for Harry S. Truman," 561.

[143] Marshall, *PGCM vol. V*, 459.

[144] US Department of State, *FRUS, 1946, vol. 9*, 1249.

[145] Caughey, *The Marshall Mission*, 25; US Department of State, *The China White Paper, August 1949* (Stanford: Stanford University Press, 1967) 686-689.

[146] US Department of State, *The China White Paper*, 688.

In the short time between 20 December 1945 and 13 January 1946, Marshall built significant momentum in achieving Truman's strategic aims. Marshall believed he could transform the initial cease-fire between the CCP and the GMD into a Political Consultative Conference that would oversee the construction of a unified military and a unified government – the only solution, in his eyes, to the crisis that threatened peace in the Pacific Theater.[147] After Marshall returned to Washington briefly in late March 1946 to secure additional loans for the Chinese Government, the brief peace began to sour as both sides sought to use the brief cessation in hostilities to maneuver to positions of advantage.[148] Marshall returned and, with the same frenetic pace as the first three weeks on the ground, by June achieved a cessation of hostilities in Manchuria and implemented a monitoring mechanism for the cease-fire. Yet the suspicion, concomitant discord, and machinations continued and Marshall realized by September that he could not convince Chiang Kai-shek that a military solution did not exist.

Conclusion: Marshall, China, and the Development of Judgment

In December 1945, George C. Marshall accepted dual and competing missions from President Truman. Truman wanted Marshall to both shepherd a unified Chinese government into place and, secretly, to continue to back the Nationalists over the Communists with the support of US military resources then available in China.[149] Despite the apparent contradiction, Marshall approached the mission with a positive outlook and the sense that he could, despite enormous

---

[147] Marshall, *PGCM vol. V*, 397.

[148] Ibid., 525.

[149] US Department of State, *FRUS, 1945, vol 7.* "The Marshall Mission: Instructions to General of the Army George C. Marshall Regarding United States Policy Towards China: First Conferences in China (1945)," US Government Printing Office, accessed March 24, 2014, http://digital.library.wisc.edu/1711.dl/FRUS.FRUS1945v07, 745-747; Pogue, *Marshall: Statesman*, 65-67.

obstacles, meet Truman's intent.[150] Early in his tour, though, Marshall recognized that Chiang

Kai-shek and the GMD could not defeat the Communists militarily and that the only hope for

respite from civil war lay in a unified government.[151] Marshall made this assessment with

astonishing speed and never backed away from it. Later, as Secretary of State, Marshall remained

certain in his assessment and rejected calls for US military aid. How did Marshall make this

assessment in so narrow a window and why where these impressions so lasting? Operational

considerations, and more specifically, the mission variables that refined Marshall's understanding

of the situation, formed a pattern instantly recognizable to Marshall. This pattern showed that the

GMD could not win militarily.

In his best-selling book *Blink*, Malcolm Gladwell relates an anecdote about a small group

of professional art historians who, upon viewing a statue recently acquired by a major museum

for millions of dollars, immediately and almost inexplicably knows the statue is a fake. One of the

historians said the statue made him feel "cold" and another described "intuitive repulsion."[152]

This reaction came as a surprise to the museum's curators as they had substantiated the statue's

provenance with an extensive paper trail and had even submitted the statue to tests that confirmed

the age and extract of the statue's marble. Subsequent and more diligent investigations into the

statue confirmed the instantaneous assessment made by the professional historians.[153] Gladwell

attributes the ability to make rapid and accurate assessments to "the kind of wisdom that someone

---

[150] Pogue, *Marshall: Statesman*, 75; Caughey, *The Marshall Mission*, 110.

[151] US Department of State, *FRUS, 1946, vol. 9. The Far East: China,* US Government Printing Office, accessed April 29, 2014, http://digital.library.wisc.edu/1711.dl/FRUS. FRUS1946v09, 815-817. The actual document is a telegram from General Marshall to President Truman dated 6 May 1946. Though Marshall does not stated explicitly that the KMT would not defeat the Communists, Marshall notes that the KMT greatly overestimated its strength and failed in the three operations conducted during Marshall's brief absence.

[152] Malcolm Gladwell, *Blink: The Power of Thinking Without Thinking* (New York: Back Bay Books, 2007), 6-7.

[153] Ibid., 7-9.

acquires after a lifetime of learning and watching and doing."[154] Gladwell's entertaining account

of the almost instantaneous ability to evaluate a complex system only serves to refresh a concept

long known to the military as *coup d'oeil*. From the French "stroke of the eye," Carl von

Clausewitz describes *coup d'oeil* as "the quick recognition of truth that the mind... would

perceive only after long study and reflection."[155] Gary Klein, a research psychologist, describes

the same phenomenon as intuition. Two critical points in Klein's analysis include the genesis of

intuition in experience and the use of this experience "to recognize key patterns that indicate the

dynamics of the situation."[156] When he landed in Shanghai on 20 December 1945, Marshall had

been in uniform for nearly half a century; if anyone could recognize patterns in an activity as

complex as war, Marshall could.[157]

Moreover, Marshall was no neophyte to either Asia or China, nor was he unfamiliar with

the Chinese way of warfare. In fact, the context in which Marshall conducted operations in China

of the 1920s bore striking similarities to the operational environment of the 1940s. Marshall

himself stated as much when he met with senior Nationalists in April 1946: "I was here when the

present situation got underway... in 1927. I have sat in the middle the past few months and

watched the situation develop. I believe I know what I'm talking about."[158] The similarity

explains why the set of lessons he took from his time in China in the 1920s weighed on his

judgment in the 1940s. Marshall's experiences in his capacity as commander and executive

---

[154] Ibid., 260.

[155] Carl von Clausewitz, *On War* (Princeton, NJ: Princeton University Press, 1976), 102.

[156] Gary Klein, *Sources of Power: How People Make Decisions* (Cambridge, MA: The MIT Press, 1999), 33, 31.

[157] Pogue, *Interviews and Reminiscences*, ix. Clausewitz established his bona fides to discuss war by citing "years of thinking about war, much association with able men who knew war, and a good deal of personal experience with it..." Clausewitz, *On War*, 62.

[158] *FRUS, 1946, vol. 9*, 789-790.

officer of the 15th Infantry Regiment in Tianjin from September 1924 to May 1927 provided the lens through which he viewed the operational environment of the 1940s.[159]

In the 1920s, the critical lessons Marshall gleaned highlighted the limits of American power in Asia. Marshall learned of America's ambivalent relationship towards imperialism and the concomitant visceral Chinese reaction to foreign intervention. He had a front row seat to a civil war fought fiercely behind opaque political walls as well as on the battlefield. He learned that foreigners were wise to "avoid violent phases" of internecine Chinese warfare.[160] Marshall believed that should a strongman seize power and address the population's needs, that this leader could control China's interior and set terms for foreigners. Finally, Marshall relearned a fundamental lesson of the conduct of warfare: the critical importance of protecting one's lines of communication. These lessons framed both how Marshall saw the problem in China and his operational approach with Chiang and Mao in the 1940s.

The conclusion that operational considerations proved definitive in Marshall's decision to terminate the mission runs counter to the conventional explanation. The conventional explanation, as described in the introduction, focuses on the strategic implications of Marshall's decision to terminate his mission. In the positive view, Marshall withheld American military support because he knew that a Chinese civil war would become a quagmire and that every dollar, or piece of equipment, or troop used in Asia would subtract from the Marshall Plan in Europe. And in the negative view, Marshall simply did not understand China's geostrategic importance. In fact, no less than Lieutenant General Albert C. Wedemeyer, the commander of US Forces China Theater during Marshall's mission and a trusted former subordinate, believed Marshall did not understand

---

[159] Marshall, *PGCM vol. I*, 264. The citation is for the dates of his service in Tianjin.

[160] Marshall, *PGCM vol. I*, 294.

the operational environment.[161] Wedemeyer wrote in 1958 that Marshall simply did not understand the threat of Soviet communism and that, "the United States… had no other resource but to support Chiang Kai-shek and his government."[162] This view, though, rests on the premise that American military effort could have somehow changed the fundamental situation. Marshall disagreed.

When President Harry Truman left office in 1953 and began his memoirs, he wrote to Marshall to ask for a summary of his mission to China.[163] Marshall's response includes an explanation for why the mission ultimately failed. He writes:

> Always in my conversations with [Chiang Kai-shek] I put forward my military opinion that the use of force at that time by the Nationalist Government could not be productive of more success than that of the capture of cities – that the long lines of communication made military operations for the Nationalist Government far more difficult than they were prepared to meet. So long as the Communists confined themselves to attacks on the line of communications and the break down of the influence of the Nationalist Government with the Chinese people, their eventual success seems to me to be assured.[164]

The historical record does not reveal precisely when Marshall concluded a Nationalist military victory unlikely. Marshall famously kept his own council about his personal views, especially when those views might constrain his superior's options.[165] But that he did come to this conclusion explains why, after returning from the failed mission, he refused to entertain notions of commitment of US forces in the region. Marshall recognized a pattern in which

---

[161] Marshall, *PGCM vol. II*, 518; *vol. IV*, 579; *vol. V*, 390. Citation establishes Wedemeyer's position and that he was a trusted subordinate.

[162] Albert C. Wedemeyer, *Wedermeyer Reports!* (New York: Holt, 1958), 368.

[163] Marshall, "Memorandum for Harry S. Truman," 560.

[164] Marshall, "Memorandum for Harry S. Truman," 565-566.

[165] Mark A. Stoler, *George C. Marshall: Soldier-Statesman of the American Century* (Boston: Twayne Publishers, 1989), 86.

accomplishing a military objective could not meet the strategic end state and with a stroke of the eye, he saw the way forward.

The primacy of operational considerations in Marshall's decisions of 1947 implies not only that strategic leaders must consider the operational level before making strategic decisions, but that sound strategic decision-making relies fundamentally on an accurate evaluation of operational considerations. If this statement appears uncontroversial then its implication for military education should seem similarly noncontentious: one cannot attain mastery in strategic studies until one first masters operational studies. Yet the US Army War College no longer requires its students to work through operational problems as part of its strategic curriculum.[166] This departure would likely surprise Marshall who, immediately following his time in Tianjin in 1927, instructed at the War College and focused on providing the students with "guidance and experience in commanding large units… to develop their decision-making skills."[167] Marshall's judgment, his ability to visualize and direct a way forward, relied on his operational understanding; strategic curricula at senior military service schools would likely benefit from the inclusion of operational problem-solving.

---

[166] US Army War College, Army War College Curriculum Summary, accessed October 14, 2014, http://www.carlisle.army.mil/orgs/SSL/DNSS/.

[167] Marshall, *PGCM vol. I*, 294.

Bibliography

Primary Sources

Beal, John Robinson. *Marshall In China*. Garden City, NY: Doubleday, 1970.

Caughey, John Hart. *The Marshall Mission to China, 1945-1947: The Letters and Diary of Colonel John Hart Caughey*, edited by Roger B. Jeans. Lanham, MD: Rowman & Littlefield Publishers, Inc., 2011.

Connelly, Mathew J. Oral History Interview conducted August 21, 1968. Harry S. Truman Library Website. Accessed September 1, 2014. http://www.trumanlibrary.org/oralhist/connly3.htm.

Connor, William D. to Adjutant General and G-2 Division, War Department, General Staff United States Army. "Notes on visit to Marshal Wu Pei Fu's Headquarters," June 4, 1924. Reel 5, Document 0325 in *China, 1911-1941 [microfilm]: U.S. Military Intelligence Reports*, United States War Department, Military Intelligence Division, edited by Paul Kesaris and Lester, Robert, 1983.

General Marshall's Daily Appointments 27 November 1945 – 21 January 1947. In *George C. Marshall's Mediation Mission to China*, edited by Larry I Bland, 596-616. Lexington, VA: George C. Marshall Research Foundation, 1998.

Marshall, George C. *Memoirs of My Services in the World War: 1917-1918*. Boston: Houghton Mifflin Company, 1976.

———. "Memorandum for Harry S. Truman on the China Mission, 17 May 1954." In *George C. Marshall's Mediation Mission to China*, edited by Larry I Bland, 560-567. Lexington, VA: George C. Marshall Research Foundation, 1998.

———. *The Papers of George Catlett Marshall, Volume I*, edited by Larry I. Bland and Sharon R. Ritenour. Baltimore: The Johns Hopkins University Press, 1981.

———. *The Papers of George Catlett Marshall, Volume II*, edited by Larry I. Bland, Sharon R. Ritenour, and Clarence E. Wunderlin, Jr. Baltimore: The Johns Hopkins University Press, 1986.

———. *The Papers of George Catlett Marshall, Volume III*, edited by Larry I. Bland and Sharon Ritenour Stevens. Baltimore: The Johns Hopkins University Press, 1991.

———. *The Papers of George Catlett Marshall, Volume IV*, edited by Larry I. Bland and Sharon Ritenour Stevens. Baltimore: The Johns Hopkins University Press, 1996.

———. *The Papers of George Catlett Marshall, Volume V*, edited by Larry I. Bland and Sharon Ritenour Stevens. Baltimore: The Johns Hopkins University Press, 2003.

———. *The Papers of George Catlett Marshall, Volume VI*, edited by Larry I. Bland, Mark A. Stoler, and Sharon Ritenour Stevens. Baltimore: The Johns Hopkins University Press, 2013.

———. *George C. Marshall: Interviews and Reminiscences for Forrest C. Pogue,* edited by Larry I. Bland and Joellen K. Bland. Lexington, VA: George C. Marshall Research Foundation, 1991.

———. *Marshall's Mission to China, December 1945-January 1957: The Report and Appended Documents.* Edited by Lyman P. Van Slyke. Arlington, VA: University Publications of America, 1976.

Peterkin, Wilbur J. *Inside China, 1943-1945: An Eyewitness Account of America's Mission in Yenan.* Baltimore: Gateway Press, 1992.

US Army Corps of Engineers, Strategic Intelligence Branch. *Hopeh-Shantung Region (China): Terrain Intelligence.* Strategic engineering study, no. 150. Washington: US Army, 1945.

US Department of State. Office of Far Eastern Affairs. *Foreign Relations of the United States, 1945, Vol. 7.* US Government Printing Office. Accessed February 24, 2014. http://digital.library.wisc.edu/1711.dl/FRUS.FRUS1945v07.

US Department of State. Office of Far Eastern Affairs. *Foreign Relations of the United States, 1946, Vol. 9.* US Government Printing Office. Accessed February 24, 2014. http://digital.library.wisc.edu/1711.dl/FRUS.FRUS1946v09.

US Department of State. *The China White Paper, August 1949.* Stanford: Stanford University Press, 1967.

Wedemeyer, Albert C. *Wedemeyer On War and Peace.* Stanford: Hoover Institution, Stanford University Press, 1987.

———. *Wedermeyer Reports!* New York: Holt, 1958.

Secondary Sources

Army Doctrine Reference Publication 3-0, *Unified Land Operations.* Washington, DC: Government Printing Office, May 2012.

Birtle, Andrew. "The Marshall Mission: A Peacekeeping Mission that Failed." *Military Review* 80, iss. 2 (March/April 2000): 99-103.

Bland, Larry I, ed. *George C. Marshall's Mediation Mission to China.* Lexington, VA: George C. Marshall Research Foundation, 1998.

Bruscino, Thomas. "Naturally Clausewitzian: U.S. Army Thoery and Education from Reconstruction to the Interwar Years." *The Journal of Military History* 77 (October 2013): 1251-1275.

Chen-main, Wang. "Marshall's Approaches to the Mediation Effort." In *George C. Marshall's Mediation Mission to China,* edited by Larry I Bland, 21-43. Lexington, VA: George C. Marshall Research Foundation, 1998.

Clausewitz, Carl von. *On War,* edited and translated by Michael Howard and Peter Paret. Princeton, NJ: Princeton University Press, 1976.

Coffman, Edward M. "The American 15th Infantry Regiment in China, 1912-1938: A Vignette in Social History." *The Journal of Military History* 58, no. 1 (January, 1994): 57-74.

Cressey, George B. *China's Geographic Foundations: A Survey of the Land and Its People.* New York: McGraw-Hill Book Company, 1934.

Feis, Herbert. *The China Tangle: the American Effort in China, From Pearl Harbor to the Marshall Mission.* Princeton: Princeton University Press, 1953.

Gregor, William J. "Military Planning Systems and Stability Operations." *Prism* 1, no. 3 (June, 2010): 99-114.

Jordan, Donald A. *The Northern Expedition: China's National Revolution of 1926-1928.* Honolulu: The University Press of Hawaii, 1976.

Kubek, Anthony. *How the Far East Was Lost: American Policy and the Creation of Communist China, 1941-1949.* Chicago: H. Regnery, 1963.

Machado, Barry F. "Undervalued Legacy: Marshall's Mission to China." In *George C. Marshall: Servant of the American Nation*, edited by Charles F. Browler, 117-128. New York: Palgrave Macmillan, 2011.

May, Ernest R. "1947-48: When Marshall Kept the U.S. Out of War in China." *Journal of Military History* 66, iss. 4 (October, 2002): 1001-1010.

McCullough, David. *Truman.* New York, Simon & Schuster, 1992.

McDougall, Walter A. *Promised Land, Crusader State: The American Encounter with the World Since 1776.* New York: Houghton Mifflin, 1997.

Melby, John F. "The Marshall Mission in Retrospect." *Pacific Affairs* 50, no. 2 (Summer, 1977): 272-277.

Noble, Dennis L. *The Eagle and the Dragon: The United States Military in China, 1901-1937.* New York: Greenwood Press, 1990.

Preston, Diana. *The Boxer Rebellion: The Dramatic Story of China's War on Foreigners that Shook the World in the Summer of 1900.* New York: Walker Publishing, 1999.

Pogue, Forrest C. *George C. Marshall: Statesman.* New York: Viking Penguin, 1987.

Reist, Katherine K. Review of *The Marshall Mission To China, 1945-1947: The Letters and Diary of Colonel John Hart Caughey*, edited by Roger Jeans. *Journal of Military History* 76, iss. 3 (July 2012): 921-922.

Spence, Jonathan D. *The Search for Modern China.* New York: W.W. Norton & Company, 1990.

Stewart, Richard W., ed. *American Military History, Vol. II.* Washington, DC: US Army Center of Military History, 2010.

Stoler, Mark A. *George C. Marshall: Soldier-Statesman of the American Century*. Boston: Twayne Publishers, 1989.

———. "The Marshall Legacy." In *George C. Marshall: Servant of the American Nation*, edited by Charles F. Browler, 173-184. New York: Palgrave Macmillan, 2011.

Sun, Yuemei. "The Third Force in the Marshall Mission." Master's thesis, University of Georgia, 2000.

Tsou, Tang. *America's Failure in China, 1941-50*. Chicago: University of Chicago Press, 1967.

Tuchman, Barbara W. *Stillwell and the American Experience in China, 1911-1945*. New York: Bantam Books, 1972.

US Army War College. Army War College Curriculum Summary. Accessed October 14, 2014 http://www.carlisle.army.mil/orgs/SSL/DNSS/.

US Department of State. Office of the Historian. *United States Relations with China: Boxer Uprising to Cold War (1900-1949)*. US Government Printing Office. Accessed August 1, 2014. http://2001-2009.state.gov/r/pa/ho/pubs/fs/90689.htm.

Von Plinsky, Alexander, H. "Albert C. Wedemeyer's Missions in China, 1944-1947: An Attempt to Achieve the Impossible." Master's thesis, U.S. Army Command and General Staff College, Ft. Leavenworth, Kansas, 1991.

Waldron, Arthur. *From War to Nationalism: China's Turning Point, 1924-1925*. New York: Cambridge University Press, 1995.

Westad, Odd Arne. *Decisive Encounters: The Chinese Civil War, 1946-1950*. Stanford: Stanford University Press, 2003.

Wu, Jiaqing. "The Marshall Mission and the KMT-CCP Negotiations after World War II." Master's thesis, Michigan State University, 1984.

Yu, Maochun. *The Dragon's War: Allied Operations and the Fate of China, 1937-1947*. Annapolis, MD: Naval Institute Press, 2006.

www.ingramcontent.com/pod-product-compliance
Lightning Source LLC
Chambersburg PA
CBHW081537280526
45788CB00010B/3262